T T Centenary Souvenir Edition
compiled by Geoff Cannell and John Watterson

Often described as the Everest of motorcycling, the Tourist Trophy Races have endured a chequered existence over the past century.

The average speed may have gone up from 42mph to 129mph, but the basic principle of the TT remains precisely the same 100 years after the first event.

The development of machines for road use by racing them over the demanding roads of the Isle of Man is as much a challenge now as it was in 1907.

Starting out in 1905 as trials for the British team taking part in the International Cup in France, the Island's races soon became universally accepted as the ultimate test of man and machine. Often threatened with extinction, they have survived to rightfully earn their place at the Road Racing Capital of the World.

The first four years of the motorcycle TT were run on a 15-mile course based on the central Island village of St John's, directly in the shadow of Tynwald Hill, where the Island's parliament assembles annually to proclaim its new laws.

Winners of the first races on Monday, May 28, 1907 were Rem Fowler (Norton twin) and Charlie Collier (Matchless single) at 42.91mph and 41.81mph respectively. Twenty-five riders took part in conditions which were difficult throughout, with pedalling employed to ascend Creg Willy's Hill above Glen Helen. 670cc twin-cylinder 10-lap race which had attracted 83 entries.

1907: An early dare-devil TT rider trails his right leg to stay upright as he rounds the Devil's Elbow on the Peel Coast Road. Road surfaces were poor and often included nails discarded from horses' hooves!

Writing in the Bemsee magazine 50 years later in 1957, Rem Fowler had this to say: "As I look back to that rather dreary and damp morning of May 28, 1907, little did I realise what we were starting! There were our numbered pegs in the grass verge under the back wall of the Tynwald Inn, with the starting line chalked across the road; complete with two tables borrowed from the above, at which presided the secretary and other Auto-Cycle Union officials, with their clocks, etc.

"We did not realise that from these humble beginnings would grow the TT as known today. This, in my opinion, is the finest and best organised event of its kind in the world, and has done more than anything else to put us in the forefront in everything pertaining to motorbikes, not forgetting accessories."

The St John's Course was used again in 1908, 1909 and 1910, with the lap record left at 53.15mph by H. H. Bowen (BAT) in the combined 500cc single cylinder and 670cc twin-cylinder 10-lap race which had attracted 83 entries.

1908: Competitors assemble for the start at St John's. The area now forms part of the car park of the Tynwald Inn.

1909: A roadside fuel fill-up in the third year of the TT.

1910: Speeds of nearly 60mph were reached as riders battled along the Kirk Michael to Peel Coast Road at Lynague.

Plenty of street furniture hazards at the Albany Road junction in Peel. 1910 it was the last time the original course was used. The rider is H. L. Cooper (Triumph).

The TT moved to the Snaefell Mountain Course in 1911. Remarkably, the lap speeds proved in a similar region as the course's predecessor, with Oliver Godfrey leading home a clean sweep by the American-made Indian team, though the fastest lap was by Frank Phillip (Scott) at 50.11mph.

There were three more years of TT racing on the Mountain Course before the First World War, with the lap record eventually left at 53.50mph by H. O. Wood (Scott) when winning the 1914 Senior.

When racing resumed, a section of the course was replaced. Instead of going via Johnny Watterson's Lane and Ballanard Road, riders kept straight on at Cronk-ny-Mona and went through Signpost Corner, Bedstead, the Nook and Governor's Bridge. It set the pattern for a course that remains basically unaltered today.

The grandstand, scoreboards and pits were originally a little farther down the road than today, but the set-up established a layout that has stood the test of time for 87 years.

Tommy de la Hay (Sunbeam) won the first post-War Senior, averaging 40.53mph for the seven laps, with great TT character George Dance doing the fastest lap at 55.62mph.

A year later in 1921 there was something of a sensation when Howard Davies won the Senior race on a 350cc AJS, defeating the 500cc Indians of Dixon and Le Vack. It wasn't until many years later that a 350cc beat the big bikes when the nimble 351cc TZ Yamahas beat their bigger cousins by virtue of one fewer refuelling stop.

Stanley Woods started his career in 1922 and came to notice straightaway by insisting on continuing even though he and his 250cc Cotton burst into flames at the pits. He took fifth place and was on his way to 10 victories before the Second World War.

A sidecar event came to the programme in 1923, won by Freddie Dixon, who also went on to win the 1927 Junior and thus became the only man to win two and three-wheeler TTs – he still is! But the sidecars lasted only three years until they were brought back in 1954.

Jimmy Simpson (AJS) set the first 60mph lap in the 1924 Junior and later was the first to lap at more than 70mph (1926 Senior AJS) and 80mph (1931 Senior Norton) but failed to win any of the three. Ironically, his sole TT win was to be the 1934 Lightweight on a Rudge. 1924 also saw a mass start for the 175cc Ultra Lightweight won by Jock Porter (New Gerrard).

The first TT double came in 1925 when Walter Handley took the Junior and Ultra Lightweight races on Rex Acme machines. A year later the Italian Pietro Ghersi (Moto Guzzi) was disqualified from second place in the Lightweight after using a spark plug of a different make from that declared on his scrutineering form. He was allowed to keep his 63.12mph lap record.

1912: This competitor takes no chances as he whizzes through Keppel Gate and contemplates the high-speed drop to Creg-ny-Baa. This corner later became known as Kate's Cottage.

BBC Radio introduced live radio commentaries in 1927 and three years later told listeners of Jimmie Guthrie's first TT win – the Lightweight on an AJS. In 1932 the Duke of Kent gave the TT the royal touch with a flying visit.

As the war clouds began to gather, there was a sensational Senior TT when Stanley Woods (Guzzi) snatched victory with a brave and gallant last lap that saw Guthrie (Norton) lose the win by some smart tactics by the wily Irishman. Many fans missed seeing it, having to return home when, for the first time, weather caused a day's postponement.The first foreign TT win was recorded by Italian Omobono Tenni (Guzzi) in the 1937 Lightweight and in the Senior Freddie Frith (Norton) put the lap record over 90mph.

Twelve months later Harold Daniell (Norton) lapped under 25 minutes to win the Senior and left the pre-Second World War lap record at precisely 91mph.

The 1939 Senior gave a foretaste of what was around the corner when Georg Meier won on a supercharged BMW and gave the Nazi salute at the prize-giving. War was only three months away.

The start and finish area was moved from the top of Bray Hill to Quarter Bridge Road in 1913, but cunningly far enough along to prevent riders out of fuel coasting down Bray Hill to the line! H. O. Wood wins the Senior.

Cyril Pullin (Rudge) won the last Senior before the First World War.

1920: Manxman Doug Brown astride his Norton prior to the race.

Warily taking the loose surfaced Creg-ny-Baa watched by a large crowd.

1922: The hairpin turn at Governor's Bridge holds no fears for this pair.

1923: The first Manxman to win a TT - Tom Sheard (Douglas).

It's certainly no longer allowed, but sidecars and solos used to often tangle.

1924: The mass start of the Ultra Lightweight won by Jock Porter (New Gerrard).

1925: Howard Davies displays his Senior winning home-tuned HRD.

Junior race start with Freddie Dixon (6) and Tommy de la Hay (7) in 1925 (Morton Media Archive).

1926: Len Randles and Tommy Simister take the Bungalow S-Bend.

Junior race competitors make ready for the start in 1926.

Health and Safety was not a major issue in the early years of racing on the Mountain Course. Here, dozens of spectators stand on the outside of the bend at Ballacraine as two competitors hurtle past (Morton Media Archive).

1927: The start of the 1927 Senior TT won by Alec Bennett (Norton).

1928: Alec Bennett broke lap and race records in his Junior win on a Velocette (Stafford Johns/Alan Kelly Collection)

1929: Speeding through Kirk Michael S. P. Jackson (250 Montgomery).

H. G. Tyrell-Smith comes a cropper at Glen Helen. After treatment in the pub he re-mounted and carried on to finish third in the 1929 Senior! (Mylrea, Peel).

Freddie Hicks (AJS) comes a cropper at Quarter Bridge (Motor Cycle).

Tim Hunt (Norton) chases R. D. Gelling (Husqvarna) at Ballacraine in 1931 (Motor Cycle).

Walter Handley well down to it on his way to third place in the 1932 Lightweight.

...son (New Imperial) exits Ramsey hairpin followed by Gunther Kalch on

Stanley Woods sensationally defeated Jimmie Guthrie by four seconds in the 1935 Senior. The Norton team thought they had it won and slowed Guthrie, but Woods spurted and grabbed it for Guzzi.

1936: H.G. Tyrell-Smith (Excelsior) runner-up in the Lightweight race. He later became a trade representative for Girling suspension.

1937: The first Italian to win a TT – Omobono Tenni (250 Moto Guzzi).

1938: Harold Daniell crosses Parliament Square leading the Senior race.

1939: Georg Meier flies the supercharged BMW over St Ninian's Crossroads, winning the Senior for the Third Reich.

When TT racing resumed in 1947 (the Manx Grand Prix amateur meeting resumed in 1946) not all the pre-War stars were on the line. Some had retired, others had been killed or wounded in the hostilities. Freddie Frith, Bob Foster, Harold Daniell and Maurice Cann were among those who returned, joined by MGP graduates such as Ken Bills and Ernie Lyons. Foster (Velocette) won the Junior and Daniell (Norton) the Senior, but speeds were down because of fuel mix restrictions. A Clubman's TT was also introduced, with its classes won by Eric Briggs (Senior Norton), Denis Parkinson (Junior Norton) and Bill McVeigh (Lightweight Triumph).

In 1949 ACU patron Prince Philip, Duke of Edinburgh, waved Daniell away as No. 1 in the Senior race, which he won after Les Graham suffered mechanical trouble in the final mile. The TT also counted towards the new FIM World Championship, which continued until taken to Silverstone in 1977 as the championship moved away from public road venues.

As the century approached its halfway point a new young rider was making his mark. Geoff Duke won the Clubman's TT and Senior Manx Grand Prix in the same year (1949) and was snapped up by Norton. He was second to Artie Bell in the 1950 Junior TT before really establishing himself by winning the Senior - three Mountain Course victories within the space of 12 months.

It was the start of an Island career that continued until 1959 and yielded four more Mountain Course victories – Seniors in 1951 and 1955 and Juniors in 1951 and 1952. His retirement with clutch trouble in the 1952 Senior left a great race between Reg Armstrong (Norton) and Les Graham (MV Agusta). Graham led but encountered transmission trouble, while Armstrong had to replace his back chain on the last lap. Armstrong won, truly enjoying the luck of the Irish by getting over the line just as the primary chain broke!

Manliff Barrington (Moto Guzzi) wins the 1947 Lightweight race.

Artie Bell benefits from Omobono Tenni's trouble and takes his second successive Senior in 1948.

1949: HRH Prince Philip, Duke of Edinburgh, chats to Harold Daniell before the start.

1950: The immaculate riding style of Geoff Duke as he takes Quarter Bridge in his Senior winning ride.

1951: Dario Ambrosini takes his Benelli to second place in the Lightweight.

Scotsman Fergus Anderson gets airborn on Braddan straight on his way to winning the 1952 Lightweight on the factory Moto Guzzi (Island Photographics/Keig).

1953: Les Graham beats the field in the Ultra Lightweight race, only sadly to be killed in the Senior the following day.

1954 saw a new TT course brought into action. The 10.79-mile Clypse Course featured the 125cc Ultra Lightweight and the reintroduction of the Sidecar class, the latter including the first female TT participation when Inge-Stoll Laforge passengered Jacques Drion to fifth place. Austrian Rupert Hollaus (NSU) narrowly defeated Italian Carlo Ubbiali in the 125 and Englishman Eric Oliver (Norton) fended off a large contingent of German BMW crews to win the sidecar race.

Duke won the 1955 Senior TT on a Gilera but all attention surrounded an announcement that he had done a 100mph lap. It was later corrected to 99.97mph thereby incurring the wrath of the crowds, who would have been content to see their hero forever thus titled. As it was, it was team-mate Bob McIntyre who ultimately took the honours two years later. Another mark made in 1955, and never equalled thereafter, was that of Derbyshire's Bill Lomas. He won the Junior race on the Mountain Course and the Lightweight on the Clypse - the only rider ever to win two TTs on two different courses in the same week.

John Surtees survived wrecking his best MV Agusta when he collided with a cow in an early morning practice in 1956. His spare machine was more than equal to the challenge of winning his – and MV's - first Senior TT on a very blustery day.

Then came the Golden Jubilee TT in 1957 and McIntyre did the double for Gilera, with Duke's stand-in Bob Brown from Australia third in both races. Keith Campbell (Guzzi) was runner-up in the Junior and Surtees likewise in the 500, the latter run over eight laps!

Gilera, Moto-Guzzi and Mondial all pulled out of racing at the end of that season, citing spiralling costs not reflected in resulting sales. It left the way open for MV and Surtees obliged with five wins out of his next six TTs. Mike Hailwood also joined the fray, winning replicas in all four races in his debut year 1958.

1954: Eric Oliver and Les Nutt win the first Sidecar TT since 1925. It took place over the Clypse Course.

Honda came along a year later, just in time to cut their teeth in the last year of the Clypse Course. They won the team prize in the 125cc race, but few imagined that only two years later they would sweep the board in both Lightweight classes. A Formula One race was run as a prelude to the TT but was not popular and was soon quietly dropped.

Another new decade saw sidecars come back to the Mountain Course for the first time since 1925. Helmut Fath (BMW) won, while Surtees signed off with a Senior victory after conceding the Junior to team-mate John Hartle when gearbox gremlins struck.

1961 was quite a year, with Hailwood becoming the first man to win three TTs in a week. It could have been four, but his AJS rattled to a halt as he led on the last of the seven laps. He won the Senior on a Bill Lacey-tuned Norton and gave Honda its first Isle of Man victories in the 125 and 250cc events. Sidecar passenger Marie Lambert became the first female to be killed in the TT.

Beryl Swain caused a minor sensation when her entry was accepted for the 50cc race, newly introduced to the TT programme for 1962. She completed the course on her tiny Itom. East Germany's Ernst Degner won on a Suzuki.

Japan won her first (and, so far, only) TT when Mitsuo Itoh took the honours in the 50cc race a year later. Southern Rhodesian Jim Redman started a 250-350cc treble double for Hondas and Geoff Duke brought the 1957 Gileras out of mothballs but Hartle and Phil Read could not repel Hailwood (MV) in the Senior, or Redman in the Junior. Tony Godfrey became the first rider ever to be evacuated by air ambulance when he crashed his 250cc Yamaha near Ramsey.

The TT ran in August in 1966 because of the national seamen's strike. With the Manx Grand Prix hot on its heels, there were four weeks back-to-back racing that year! Giacomo Agostini had made his entrance in 1965

Rhodesian Ray Amm drops a precautionary foot as he takes Quarter Bridge in the controversial 1954 Senior, cut short by bad weather (Manx Press Pictures).

and only a year later won the Junior. On the first time a race was run on a Sunday, Fritz Scheidegger (BMW) won the sidecars only to be disqualified for using a different make of fuel from that specified on his entry form. He was later reinstated.

The Diamond Jubilee in 1967 included a fantastic Senior scrap between Agostini and Hailwood, resolved only when the Italian's back chain broke at Windy Corner when narrowly in the lead. A Le Mans-type start was used for a Production race won by Hartle (750cc), Neil Kelly (500cc) and Bill Smith (250cc). It was only the third TT win by a Manxman (Kelly).

Barry Sheene rode in the 1971 event but failed to distinguish himself and pronounced that it was "not for him" as the groundswell of opinion against true road races began to gather pace. And when Italian Gilberto Parlotti was killed in the 1972 125 race, Agostini, Read and Sheene had the ammunition they needed to stop the TT continuing as the British round of the World Championship. It took four more years' campaigning before Silverstone became its new home. The final Isle of Man round was the 1976 250cc race won by Tom Herron. A then-unknown called Joe Dunlop was also shown on the entry list – a humble start for the man destined to win 26 TTs.

1955: Crowd idol Geoff Duke takes the four-cylinder Gilera to victory in the Senior but was robbed of the 100mph lap by a timekeeping error.

1956: Londoner John Surtees gained his and MV Agusta's maiden Senior TT victory having lost the Junior when he ran out of petrol on the last lap.

1957: Glaswegian Bob McIntyre completes the Golden Jubilee Junior-Senior double on the fabulous four-cylinder Gileras from Arcore in Italy. His week was best remembered for the first official 100mph lap of the Snaefell Mountain Course.

Dickie Dale rides the complex eight-cylinder Moto Guzzi to fourth place in the eight-lap Senior race of 1957 – a distance of over 300 miles (Kirton).

1958: Diminutive Carlo Ubbiali again demonstrated his mastery of the Lightweight classes by winning on the Clypse Course. Here he is on the 250cc MV Agusta.

A very youthful Mike Hailwood wins the second of his four silver replicas he took in his debut year in 1958. This is the 250cc race where he rode an NSU to third (Kirton).

Florian Camathias and Helmar Cecco slide the flat-twin BMW outfit round Parkfield on the final sidecar race over the Clypse Course in 1959. They finished second to Walter Schneider and Hans Strauss (Kirton).

1960: John Surtees had ironed the bugs out of the big MV Agustas and had little trouble winning the Junior and Senior races. This is the 500cc event.

Australian Tom Phillis was one of the first non-Asian riders to be awarded a factory Honda in 1960. But he was out of luck in the Lightweight (Kirton).

1961: Mike Hailwood became the first rider to win three TTs in a week when he signed off with a marvellous win in the Senior on a Norton tuned by Bill Lacey.

1962: Gary Hocking (MV Agusta) bettered his second place to Mike Hailwood in the Junior with victory in the 500cc category.

1963: John Hartle lapped at over 105mph on the comeback of Gileras under the banner of Scuderia Duke, but he and Phil Read could not keep with Mike Hailwood's MV in the Senior. Hartle was second and Read third.

1964: Jim Redman did the Junior-Lightweight double three years in a row.

Phil Read and the two-stroke Yamaha twins racked up many wins and world championships (Kirton).

Creg Willy's failed to deter Mike Hailwood. He kicked the MV straight and continued on to win another Senior.

Wally Rawlings take Ballaugh Bridge on their BMW in 1965 but were forc... mechanical trouble (Kirton).

1966: Bill Ivy was one of the real characters of road racing, but very talented too. Here he rounds Ramsey Hairpin on the 250-4 in the Lightweight race (Geoff Cannell).

1967: Things went sadly wrong for 25th birthday boy Giacomo Agostini when the back chain on his MV broke while battling hard with Mike Hailwood in the Senior race. He coasted in to the finish, to be sportingly told by Hailwood he would probably have had to settle for second had not his rival stopped.

1968: Siegfried Schauzu and passenger Horst Schneider drift their BMW round the Quarter Bridge on their way to victory in the 500cc class.

John Hartle's last TT was a recall by MV Agusta for the Senior in 1968. But it ended badly when he crashed at Cronk-ny-Mona as the gearbox seized (Kirton).

1969: Aussie Kel Carruthers went on to great fame as a grand prix team chief, but only after he made his name in races such as this where he won the Lightweight on a four-cylinder Benelli.

1970: Winning the TT on your debut is fairly rare, but German Dieter Braun did just that aboard his 125cc air-cooled Suzuki twin.

1971: Future World Champion Barry Sheene graced the TT for just one year and was doing well until he fell off his 125cc Suzuki at Quarter Bridge in the wet. He said he wouldn't ride in the Island again and stuck to it.

1972: Agostini's last TT – the Senior in which he and team-mate Alberto Pagani finished first and second
but vowed never to return, saying it was too dangerous after fellow Italian
Gilberto Parlotti was killed on the Verandah.

Former public schoolboy Chas Mortimer was a tidy rider on bikes of all sizes and splashed through the mist and rain to win the Ultra Lightweight race in 1972

1973: Roy Hanks followed his brother Norman and father Fred into the TT in 1966 and is still performing with distinction now, more than 40 years on. Pictured powering a BSA twin through Parliament Square, Ramsey in 1973 with passenger Gerald Daniel, Hanks has scored numerous top-six results and several podium finishes, including a win in 1997 with Phil Biggs. Roy's wife Rose also competed as a sidecar passenger, indeed she was the first woman to gain a podium finish in the TT when she finished runner-up in the 750cc event with Norman Hanks (Peter Corlett).

Australian veteran Jack Findlay delighted those Down Under by winning the 1973 Senior on a 500 Suzuki twin.

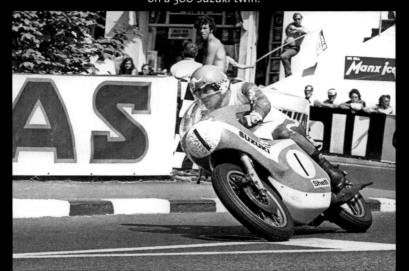

1974: Phil Carpenter surprised many with his skill and daring to win the very wet Senior on an over-bored 350cc Yamaha twin. He is pictured second left.

1975: Gritty Yorkshireman Mick Grant was always a hard TT trier and rode this 500cc Kawasaki triple to Senior victory at 100.52mph and fastest lap at 102.93mph.

Phil Read swallowed his pride by returning to the TT in 1977 and won the FIM World Formula One Championship (a single race series!) on a Honda. Dunlop rocketed to instant stardom by winning the Schweppes Jubilee Classic on a battered 750cc Yamaha-4.

Just a year later, Mike Hailwood delighted his legions of loyal fans by returning to the TT and defeating Read in a never-to-be-forgotten Formula One. His speed after an absence of 11 years staggered his opponents, though the Martini Yamahas let him down in his other races.

Hailwood was back in 1979 and won his 14th TT - the Senior on an RG Suzuki. In his last ever TT he lost out to Alex George by three seconds in the Classic. Mike was killed driving a Rover when a wagon pulled across in front of him at Tanworth-in-Arden, Warwickshire in March 1981.

His nine-year-old daughter Michelle also died, but his son David survived.

An attempt to attract international classic bikes was unsuccessful in 1984, but it gave New Yorker Dave Roper the chance to record the USA's only TT win when he rode Team Obsolete's G50 Matchless to victory in the first and only Historic TT.

A new Grandstand was built for 1986 but the year was marred by an horrific crash in which Irishman Gene McDonnell was killed when he struck a pony that had strayed on to the course at Ballaugh.

Hawick's Steve Hislop took the first of what was to be 11 TT wins in 1987 and there was the first cancellation of a TT when bad weather bedevilled the 1500cc Production.

Joey Dunlop and his pals almost went down with their fishing boat Tor-na-Mona when it sank on the way to the Isle of Man for the 1988 TT but it didn't faze the Ballymoney brigade and Joey went on to emulate Hailwood's 1961 feat by taking three victories in a single meeting.

1976: Cheshire's John Williams blitzed the TT lap record to 112.27mph but heartbreak awaited when the gearbox seized on the last corner and he was forced to push his Suzuki in as Tom Herron roared by to win the Senior.

From then on, Joey was unstoppable, winning in 125, 250, 500, 750 and 1000cc categories.

Honda celebrated 30 years since its 1961 double by sending special RVF factory bikes direct from Japan for Hislop and Carl Fogarty in 1991 but promptly issued warning notices for them not to risk themselves too much in their rivalry to be the first to lap at 125mph. Hislop won both main races, lapping at 123.48mph in the process.

Twelve months on and Hislop found himself without bikes! A last-minute deal was done for him to ride a Rotary Norton and he grabbed victory from Fogarty (Yamaha) in a thrilling Senior TT which concluded the week in 1992.

Meanwhile, sidecar racing moved from open-class 750s to Formula Two 350s, where Dave Saville, Mick Boddice, Roy Hanks and Co. were kings. Later came Dave Molyneux and Rob Fisher, who really made the newer 600s fly. Molyneux eventually broke the 20-minute barrier and went on to clock 11 wins by 2005.

Philip McCallen achieved another TT milestone in 1996 by winning four of the five races he entered, while in 2000 fellow Ulsterman Joey Dunlop again took three - just a month before he was killed racing in Estonia.

The threat of foot-and-mouth disease meant no TT was run in 2001 and in 2003 TT critics were out in force again when new star David Jefferies was killed at Crosby in an afternoon practice session.

However, the TT regained its composure and John McGuinness lapped at 129mph in 2006 to show the light continues to burn brightly with riders and spectators.

Tom Herron wins the last-ever World Championship TT race on his 250cc Yamaha twin in 1976. The Japanese rider Takazumi Katayama was second as the curtain closed on the Isle of Man as a venue for the FIM world series which transferred to Silverstone.

1977: Phil Read put aside earlier reservations about TT safety and won the new Formula One class on a factory-backed Honda. The Formula Two was won by Alan Jackson and the Formula Three by John Kidson.

1978: Was all about Mike Hailwood's fairy tale TT comeback. Eleven years after he last rode in the TT he returned with a Formula One Ducati and was never headed. But Yamahas in his other races were not so good (Geoff Cannell).

Californian Pat Hennen was going well in his second year at the TT in 1978, but crashed heavily at Bishop's Court in the Senior and received injuries which prevented him riding again (Geoff Cannell).

1979: Mike Hailwood's 14th and last TT win – the Senior which he took on a 500cc RG Suzuki four-cylinder two-stroke. He upped the lap record to 114.02mph and almost won his last Island race, dipping out to Alex George by less than four seconds after 226 miles of close racing.

Alex George and Mike Hailwood slugged it out for all six laps of the 1979 Open Classic with the Scot, pictured here on his 998cc Honda-4, inching home the winner.

1980: Chester's Charlie Williams recorded the last of his eight TT wins in the 1980 Junior. All of his successes came on 250 and 350cc Yamaha twins.

1981: All the way from Auckland came Graeme Crosby, but it was worth it as he won the Senior and Open Classic races for Suzuki. He went on to become a Grand Prix regular for the Suzuki and Yamaha factory teams. Controversy surrounded his F1 battle, with Honda claiming he had over-used gamesmanship. He just laughed it off.

1982: Northern Ireland's Norman Brown was a sensation on his 500cc Suzuki after making his Mountain Course debut in the Manx Grand Prix nine months earlier. He won the Senior TT despite the presence of many more experienced hands.

1983. Irishman Con Law was in fine form in the Junior race, which this year catered for lightweight bikes. He took Dr Joe Ehrlich's EMC to victory at record lap and race speeds, overcoming Graeme McGregor and Norman Brown.

1984: Rob McElnea added TT victory to his already excellent pedigree in racing and trials by winning the Senior TT on a Suzuki. He later went on to become a fully-fledged works GP rider for Marlboro Yamaha.

Ballymoney's Joey Dunlop became only the second rider to win three TTs in a week (the first was Mike Hailwood in 1961) when he took the Formula One, Senior and Junior events on Hondas in 1985. He is pictured being greeted by ACU TT chairman Vernon Cooper at the prize presentation at the Villa Marina.

Phil Mellor showed his mastery of Mona's Isle by romping a GSX-R Suzuki to Production class success at record lap and race speeds. But it was this class which later cost him his life when he high-sided at the high-speed left handed Doran's Bend three years later. He was a popular Yorkshireman who never gave less than 100 per cent commitment.

Mick Boddice, son of 1950s TT star Bill Boddice, was always a force to be reckoned with on the Mountain Course and remained competitive when the sidecar's specification was moved from 750cc to 350cc then on to 600cc.

1988: Steve Cull put in many an accomplished ride at the TT and even found time to reserve a place in the record books by winning the only 350cc Historic TT in 1984. Here he is seen at Ramsey Hairpin on the 500cc Honda triple upon which he established a new outright lap record at 119.08mph.

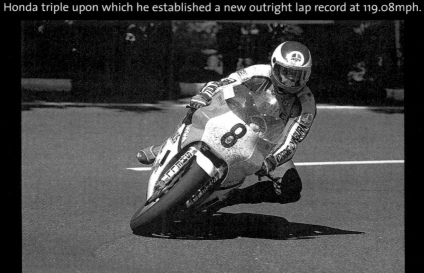

Hawick's Steve Hislop liked the Isle of Man so much he moved to live there. Along the way he recorded the first-ever 120mph lap and took a total of 11 individual race wins. An accomplished superbike rider at British and World Championship level, he lost his life in a helicopter crash in the Borders in July 2003 (Doug Baird).

1990: Dave Leach won five TTs, including the Supersport 400cc event on a V&M Yamaha in 1990 (John Watterson).

Carl Fogarty achieved great TT fame before moving on to become World Superbike Champion on Ducati's. Here is at Quarter Bridge on his works RC30 Honda on his way to winning the 1990 Formula One race.

Welshman Ian Lougher produced a stunning lap of 117.80mph on the reverse-cylinder 250cc Yamaha on his way to winning the 1990 Junior 350 race (John Watterson).

1991: Trevor Nation pictured at the Bungalow, a tricky S-Bend where competitors cross a set of railway lines! His machine is the rorty Rotary Norton ridden also by Steve Cull, Robert Dunlop, Steve Hislop and Simon Buckmaster (John Watterson).

A fabulous shot of the Honda team wheelying over the top of Lambfell and out onto the Cronk-y-Voddy Straight in the 1991 Formula One. Carl Fogarty (8), Nick Jefferies (7) and Steve Hislop (11) (John Watterson).

1992: Steve Hislop recorded a memorable win over Carl Fogarty in the Senior TT, the Scot giving Norton its first win in the race since Mike Hailwood in 1961. Here he wheelies over Agos's leap with the rotary machine doing 170mph (John Watterson).

1993: Yorkshireman Nick Jefferies and Kiwi Robert Holden battle it out on the exit from the Gooseneck. Jefferies won the Formula One race, his only TT success (John Watterson).

1994: Robert Holden demonstrates just how quickly a single-cylinder machine can be made to go. Taking the Bungalow at 70mph he was really cranking over the little Ducati Supermono (John Watterson).

Phillip McCallen leaps Ballaugh Bridge on his way to a run of three successive Formula One race wins in 1995 (John Watterson).

1996: After the loneliness of the Snaefell Mountain run, Dave Molyneux and Peter Hill drift their Honda back into suburban Douglas near the end of another high speed lap. They won both sidecar races that year (John Watterson).

Ian Simpson flat on the tank as he makes light work of Crosby Village at maximum speed in top gear in 1996. He won three TTs over the next two years (John Watterson).

Tom Hanks takes a cautionary glance over his right shoulder to discover his passenger Steve Wilson sliding up the road, having clipped the nearside railings at Braddan Bridge and fallen out of the Windle Yamaha outfit. He received only minor injuries in the skirmish (John Watterson).

2000 B Close stuff at the Gooseneck, with Michael Rutter (9) the meat in the sandwich of Joey Dunlop (6) and Adrian Archibald (3) but ahead on corrected time. It was to be Dunlop's final race over the Mountain as he was killed in Estonia a month later (John Watterson).

Jim Moodie was best at home on a Supersport 600cc mount, as shown by his flowing style at the course's first corner Quarter Bridge in his Junior-winning ride on the V&M Yamaha in 2002 (John Watterson).

2003: New Zealander Bruce Anstey gave Triumph its first TT win since 1974 when he rode to a memorable victory in the four-lap Junior 600cc event. The Isle of Man has a half claim on the shy Kiwi as his mother was born on the island (John Watterson).

2004: The gloves are off for the last time as Robert Dunlop pulls down the shutters on an glorious TT career (John Watterson).

2005: John McGuinness wheelies across the St Ninian's road junction on his way to his first Senior victory on the AIM Yamaha (John Watterson).

Welsh veteran Nigel Davies had more than his fair share of accidents on the Mountain Course in a career spanning 15 years. He suffered a broken leg in this incident at Signpost Corner in the 2005 Superbike race (Mike Proudfoot).

2006: Making only his second appearance at the TT, Melbourne ace Cameron Donald finished a spectacular runner-up in the Senior with a stunning average speed of 128.445mph on lap two (John Watterson).

Carl Rennie lands heavily on the front wheel of his Hawk Kawasaki at Ballaugh Bridge in the 2006 Senior TT (John Watterson).

Two of the TT's all-time greats, John McGuinness is presented with the magnificent Senior trophy by Italian star Giacomo Agostini who won the same trophy five consecutive years between 1968 and 1972 (John Watterson).

Clypse Course

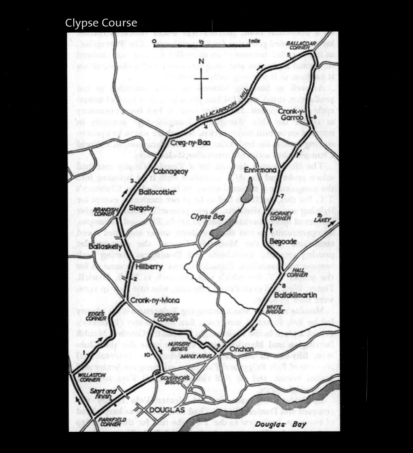